PATH OF A
BELOVED DISCIPLE

"To this you were called, because
Christ suffered for you, leaving you an
example, that you should follow
in his steps."

1 Peter 2:21

Other books by Stephen A. Macchia:

Becoming A Healthy Church

Becoming A Healthy Church Workbook

Becoming A Healthy Disciple

Becoming A Healthy Disciple: Small Group Study and Worship Guide

Becoming A Healthy Team

Becoming A Healthy Team Exercises

Crafting A Rule of Life

Wellspring: 31 Days to Whole Hearted Living

PATH OF A
BELOVED DISCIPLE

31 Days
in the Gospel of John

STEPHEN A. MACCHIA

LEADERSHIP
TRANSFORMATIONS INC.
FORMATION | DISCERNMENT | RENEWAL

Published by Leadership Transformations
P.O. Box 338, Lexington, MA 02420
www.leadershiptransformations.org

August 2014
Printed in the United States of America.

Library of Congress Cataloging-in-Publication Data
Macchia, Stephen A., 1956–
Path of a Beloved Disciple / Stephen A. Macchia.
Includes bibliographical references.
ISBN 978-0-692-27633-4 (pbk.)
Religion / Christian Life / Devotional

Unless otherwise indicated, Scripture quotations are
from The Holy Bible, English Standard Version® (ESV®),
copyright© 2001 by Crossway, a publishing ministry of Good
News Publishers. Used by permission. All rights reserved.
Cover photo by John Meinen.

Dedicated to

John and Lois Pierce

and the Pierce Center for Disciple-Building
at Gordon-Conwell Theological Seminary

Table of Contents

Introduction

Dear Friend,

Welcome to the delightful journey of discipleship! Jesus invites us to say an enthusiastic "Yes!" to his beckoning call: Come close, draw near, and follow me. This is exactly what John the Beloved Disciple said long ago and it's our invitation to intimacy today.

Becoming a "beloved disciple" of Jesus is the focus of the 31 reflections contained in this devotional guide. Each reading covers one of the 10 traits of a healthy disciple (taken from my book, *Becoming A Healthy Disciple*) or one of the 21 chapters of the Gospel of John which feature different portraits of Christ.

If you like what you read here, please consider ordering a copy of *Becoming A Healthy Disciple* as well as the *Small Group Study & Worship Guide* available as its companion for small group use.

God bless you in your daily discipleship with Jesus!

Coming alongside you with joy,

Steve Macchia

Founder and President
Leadership Transformations, Inc.
Author of *Becoming A Healthy Disciple*

Day 1

Experience God's Empowering Presence

Read: John 14:15-27

B ut the Helper, the Holy Spirit, whom the Father will send in my name, he will teach you all things and bring to your remembrance all that I have said to you. (v. 26 ESV)

Trait One: The healthy disciple understands the role of the Holy Spirit and lives daily with a fresh reality of his power and presence.

Christians have all sorts of excuses for not

getting involved in ministry opportunities ...

I should have shared my faith with my coworker, but I didn't want to offend her.

I could have joined the short-term mission team, but I don't have the time.

I would have helped out by teaching the Sunday school class, but I don't feel comfortable working with children.

The shoulda-coulda-woulda litany of excuses we espouse shows us how little we depend upon the ministry of the Holy Spirit. Jesus promised to send the Holy Spirit to all believers of every generation. The best part of the promise is that he delivered on it!

So, take time today to invite the Holy Spirit to work his ministry within you and watch how his gifts unfold and his fruit emerges right before your very eyes. No more excuses ... because with the Holy Spirit's empowerment you too can live more abundantly!

Pray: Lord, send your empowering Spirit into my life today!

Reflect

_____

_____

_____

_____

_____

_____

_____

_____

_____

_____

_____

_____

_____

_____

_____

_____

_____

_____

_____

_____

_____

_____

_____

_____

_____

Day 2

❧

Engage in God-Exalting Worship

Read: John 4:1-26

... the true worshipers will worship the Father in spirit and truth, for the Father is seeking such people to worship him. (v. 23 ESV)

Trait Two: The healthy disciple engages wholeheartedly in meaningful, God-focused worship experiences on a weekly basis with the family of God.

"I didn't get anything out of that service" mumbled Wally the worshiper as he and his wife, Wanda, drove away from church.

Sound a tad familiar? Then you too might be entering worship with the wrong motivation. If Wally and Wanda were true worshipers, they would understand that worship is about giving, not getting.

The amazing reality, however, is that in giving we receive. Funny how that happens, isn't it? As we give ourselves back to God, he fills us with his joy. As we offer our lives as a living sacrifice, God blesses us for our obedience to his call. As we sing and pray and listen and serve, the bounty of his eternal rewards are overwhelming.

Next Sunday, enter the sanctuary with a heart's desire to do nothing but give. You will undoubtedly be amazed by how the Father's heart will sing over you with joy. In the meantime, pray that your daily time of worship will prepare you for weekly worship with the family of God!

Pray: Father, help me worship you in spirit and in truth every day.

Reflect

_____

_____

_____

_____

_____

_____

_____

_____

_____

_____

_____

_____

_____

_____

_____

_____

_____

_____

_____

_____

_____

_____

_____

_____

Day 3

❦

Practice the
Spiritual Disciplines

Read John 15:1-8

Abide in me, and I in you. (v. 4 ESV)

Trait Three: The healthy disciple pursues the daily disciplines of prayer, Bible study, and reflection.

Lesser priorities tugging for our affection (and time) often usurp intimacy with Christ. Those alternative intimacies include climbing the corporate ladder, seeking self-fulfillment through money, sex, or influence over others, and a host of other ambitions and desires. All of them keep us from pursuing the heart of God.

When's the last time you sat quietly and reflectively in the presence of God? How long did you linger in his presence? For most Christians, practicing the spiritual disciplines feels like more work, another item to check off the daily to-do list. Don't let that happen to you.

God isn't any different from human parents. What he most longs for is an intimate relationship with all his children. The spiritual disciplines of prayer, Scripture study and reflection lead us into a deeper love of our Father. Make that your number one priority each new day and everything else will fall into place.

Today as you pray, sit a few minutes longer than usual and in the silence of the moment ask Jesus to help you keep intimacy with him your central mission in life. That's how your heart will become Christ's home today.

Pray: Draw near to me, Father, as I draw near to you in a quiet place where your Word can refresh my soul.

Reflect

_____

_____

_____

_____

_____

_____

_____

_____

_____

_____

_____

_____

_____

_____

_____

_____

_____

_____

_____

_____

_____

_____

_____

_____

_____

_____

Day 4

≈

Learn and Grow in Community

Read: John 21:1-14

So they cast it [the net], and now they were not able to haul it in, because of the quantity of fish. (v. 6 ESV)

Trait Four: The healthy disciple is involved in spiritual and relational growth in the context of a safe and affirming group of like-minded believers.

Did you ever wonder why God placed so many "one anothers" in the Bible? The New Testament exhorts us to love one another, confess our sins and pray for one another, care for and greet and encourage and bear with and serve one another (just to name a few). Could it be quite possibly that God actually intended for faith communities to learn to live out the "one anothers" today? Absolutely!

When disciples obey Jesus together, "hauling the net" is nothing short of pure joy. When the church learns how to fulfill all the "one anothers" in the context of healthy environments for spiritual growth, then the world will come to know the Savior for real.

Commit today to improving the health of your spiritual life by growing up into Christlikeness in unity with your brothers and sisters in the faith. Ask God to lead you into an affirming group of believers who will hold you accountable for obedience to Christ. Mutual accountability–remember those "one anothers"–is the key to discovering the joy of journeying in community.

Pray: Lord, help us to reach out and love one another.

Reflect

_____

_____

_____

_____

_____

_____

_____

_____

_____

_____

_____

_____

_____

_____

_____

_____

_____

_____

_____

_____

_____

_____

_____

_____

_____

_____

Day 5

⚬⚬

Commit to Loving
and
Caring Relationships

Read: John 15:9-17

This is my commandment, that you love one another as I have loved you. (v. 12 ESV)

Trait Five: The healthy disciple prioritizes the qualities of relational vitality that lead to genuine love for one another in the home, workplace, church, and community.

Genuinely loving relationships cannot exist unless people can resolve conflicts. How do you deal with conflict? For many, the response of choice is to "sweep it under the carpet" and pretend it never occurred. But that only creates a bumpy carpet in the body of Christ–not safe for the Christian walk.

Far too many relationships are filled with painful, unresolved conflicts. Forgiveness is a topic of understanding but little application. However, the only way to begin sweeping out the bumps from under the carpet is to confess our sin and seek the forgiveness of others.

If you desire to embody the abundant life of Jesus Christ, then your relationships with others need to be genuinely loving and life-giving. Hard hearts that are unwilling to seek and offer forgiveness will not receive God's mercy and forgiveness. Ask God to lead you to those you have hurt–or who have hurt you–and begin the process of reconciliation today. Do this and your walk through life will be smoother–guaranteed.

Pray: Lord, help me to lay down my life for my friends, even if it requires a forgiving heart.

Reflect

_____

_____

_____

_____

_____

_____

_____

_____

_____

_____

_____

_____

_____

_____

_____

_____

_____

_____

_____

_____

_____

_____

_____

_____

_____

Day 6

⚜

Exhibit Christlike Servanthood

Read: John 13:1-17

For I have given you an example, that you also should do just as I have done to you. (v. 15 ESV)

Trait Six: The healthy disciple practices God-honoring servanthood in every relational context of life and ministry.

Many Christians today serve others in order to be seen and acknowledged. Are you looking for some well-deserved applause for your most recent act of kindness? Think you should have received a thank-you note for visiting that shut-in?

Waiting to hear your name from the pulpit as the key individual who made your church ministry a reality?

Guess what? Give it up! It's best if you wait no longer. If your motivation for serving others is to be recognized for your generosity, then any ounce of sacrifice related to your service is gone.

When Jesus embodied the "full extent of his love" for his disciples, it was behind closed doors where no one else could see. And his act of kindness was demonstrated in the holding and washing of his disciples' feet, the lowliest of servant-worthy jobs.

Serving like Jesus means that we are willing to help others for their sake, and not our own. His example is not glamorous, but gracious and generous and godly. In your prayers today, invite Jesus to give you a loving heart to serve others in a hidden, anonymous, and sacrificial way.

Pray: Dear Jesus, help me to bring joy to your heart by serving others.

Reflect

_____

_____

_____

_____

_____

_____

_____

_____

_____

_____

_____

_____

_____

_____

_____

_____

_____

_____

_____

_____

_____

_____

_____

_____

Day 7

❧

Share the Love of Christ Generously

Read: John 3:1-21

For God so loved the world, that he gave his only Son, that whoever believes in him should not perish but have eternal life. (v. 16 ESV)

Trait Seven: The healthy disciple maximizes every opportunity to share the love of Christ, in word and deed, with those outside the faith.

What do you think makes Jesus smile? I believe it's when he sees his children loving God, loving neighbors as we love ourselves, and loving the world he gave his life to redeem–all through a love defined by our words and deeds.

The gospel of our Lord can be summarized in one word: Love. Not a syrupy kind of love that's short-lived, but an agape kind of love that's eternal. Sharing God's powerful, life-changing, no-matter-what kind of love is the mandate set before us.

Who in your world needs some serious loving today? It may be your spouse who misses your tenderness, or your child who longs for your attentiveness, or your friend who desires your closeness, or your neighbor who waits for your witness ... or the lost, lonely, or least who are dying and in need of your faithfulness.

Your outward focus of love is a reflection of your inward journey of joy. Ask Jesus to remove barriers that would restrict you from loving today. This will certainly make him smile!

Pray: May all I think, say, and do bear gracious witness of your love today.

Reflect

_____
_____
_____
_____
_____
_____
_____
_____
_____
_____
_____
_____
_____
_____
_____
_____
_____
_____
_____
_____
_____
_____
_____
_____
_____
_____
_____

Day 8

⨍

Manage Life Wisely and Accountably

Read: John 9:1-12

We must work the works of him who sent me while it is day ... (v. 4 ESV)

Trait Eight: The healthy disciple develops personal life management skills and lives within a web of accountable relationships.

Stress is the word of our time. Everyone I know understands what the word means, because they embody the word in their lifestyle. Activities, responsibilities, relationships, to-do lists, and taking care of our "stuff" seem to preoccupy our every waking moment. Gone are the slow days of sauntering through life. Fast pace is here to stay.

Life management skills are needed now more than ever. They begin with knowing our personal mission and focus. They grow from there into defining our key relationships and specific responsibilities. They lead to a deep, internal understanding of what to say yes to and when to say no. All of this within a framework of accountable friendships, trusted confidantes who will help us maintain our God-defined priorities.

Tackling this trait of discipleship health is critical to our well-being. Otherwise, life will continue as a hectic treadmill, and we won't ever jump off to assess our direction. Pray today for a fresh vision for your overstressed life. Seek a life balanced in wisdom (intellectual health), stature (physical health), favor with God (spiritual health) and favor with others (relational health) (Luke 2:52).

Pray: Father, please help me choose wisely whatever will best serve the interests of your kingdom.

Reflect

_____

_____

_____

_____

_____

_____

_____

_____

_____

_____

_____

_____

_____

_____

_____

_____

_____

_____

_____

_____

_____

_____

_____

_____

_____

Day 9

⚜

Network with the Body of Christ

Read: John 17:20-26

I in them and you in me, that they may become perfectly one, so that the world may know that you sent me and loved them even as you loved me. (v. 23 ESV)

Trait Nine: The healthy disciple actively reaches out to others within the Christian community for relationships, worship, prayer, fellowship, and ministry.

Unity. A small word with gigantic meaning. The implications of genuine spiritual unity are in direct proportion to the fulfillment of Jesus' prayer for building the kingdom of God. Jesus wants us to take part in building his kingdom. It will require that we participate prayerfully in uniting the people of God.

Unity. For Jesus' disciples, it was essential that they embrace one another's differences of background and vocation. Why would it be any different today? He's not asking us to water down the gospel in order to have feel-good connections with the diversity of all who claim to be Christians without solid biblical theology. He's inviting us to network with those who share our convictions and embody the Great Commission (Matt. 28:16-20).

Unity. If Jesus made it the focus of this chapter-long prayer (John 17), we should certainly make it a part of our prayer today. Ask God to give you a heart to discover the richness of the diversity of the body of Christ. This will lead us all into greater unity.

Pray: Help me, Lord Jesus, to strengthen the unity of the body of Christ through my love, prayers, and service.

Reflect

_____
_____
_____
_____
_____
_____
_____
_____
_____
_____
_____
_____
_____
_____
_____
_____
_____
_____
_____
_____
_____
_____
_____
_____
_____
_____
_____

Day 10

❧

Steward a Life of Abundance

Read: John 12:20-36

Truly, truly, I say to you, unless a grain of wheat falls into the earth and dies, it remains alone; but if it dies, it bears much fruit. (v. 24 ESV)

Trait Ten: The healthy disciple recognizes that every resource comes from the hand of God and is to be used generously for kingdom priorities and purposes.

In this passage Jesus is reminding his hearers that for life to emerge in them, he himself first must be willing to die. Here's how to apply this truth: For the abundant life of Christ to be lived out in us, we must consistently die to ourselves. Dying to ourselves means that we freely release everything we have been given so others may discover life for themselves.

Are you willing to die to yourself? This is the road to eternal life, the avenue called "discipleship." Healthy disciples invite the life-transforming Christ to permeate every decision they make. When we invite Christ to live through us, we open-handedly steward or manage carefully every kernel of life entrusted to our care—not for our own sake, but for God's redemptive work to be accomplished in the hearts of others.

Seeding our daily life lovingly and generously with all the resources we have will lead to the abundant life of discipleship Jesus calls us to receive.

Pray: Dear Jesus, help me develop what you've given me in time, talent, and treasure so you get a good—and eternal—return on your investment.

Reflect

_____

_____

_____

_____

_____

_____

_____

_____

_____

_____

_____

_____

_____

_____

_____

_____

_____

_____

_____

_____

_____

_____

_____

_____

_____

_____

_____

Day 11

The Son of God

Read: John 1:1-14

And the Word became flesh and dwelt among us, and we have seen his glory, glory as of the only Son from the Father, full of grace and truth. (v. 14 ESV)

Any parent would agree: the birth of a child is a miracle. Our children seem to us, at the instant of their birth, perfect creations, spotless (but wrinkled!) and a wonder to behold.

The miracle of Jesus' birth was amplified by his conception through the Holy Spirit. Jesus was truly and in every way imaginable the Son of God. He lived among us as God's greatest gift to planet earth, and to behold him was to look directly into the face of God.

When we look at the face of our children, we see reflections of ourselves. It may be in the sparkle of their eyes or the shape of their nose. In them we see our lineage unfold and our family continues to a new generation.

With the Son of God's arrival, the line of his kingdom is extended to new generations. And we have the privilege of expanding God's family by presenting Christ to the world in all the grace, truth, and glory he deserves.

Pray: Lord, give me a grateful heart for the joy and privilege of serving the Son of God as a full-fledged member of your family.

Reflect

_____
_____
_____
_____
_____
_____
_____
_____
_____
_____
_____
_____
_____
_____
_____
_____
_____
_____
_____
_____
_____
_____
_____
_____
_____
_____
_____
_____

Day 12

∽

The Son of Man

Read: John 2:1-11

His mother said to the servants, "Do whatever he tells you." (v. 5 ESV)

I vividly recall sitting at the top of the stairs, listening intently to the conversation of my parents and their guests late into the evening. Though I was supposed to be asleep, their parties intrigued me and I did not want to miss a word that was spoken.

When Jesus arrived at the wedding in Cana, his mother and disciples were invited as well. Well into the party, when the wine was all gone, Jesus instructed the servants to fill jars of water to the brim ... and by the time they were poured out for the guests it flowed as fine wine.

Any who watched and listened closely saw this miraculous transformation. For the disciples, this dramatic revealing of his glory brought about their faith in the Son of Man. Jesus had not only expressed his humanity by his presence at the wedding, but his miracle revolutionized the celebration and filled his disciples with awe.

What will it take for you to put your trust in the Son of Man today? May the eyes of your heart be open to his presence and life-transforming power. Listen intently to his words–but not just from a distance. He invites you to "come downstairs" into his very presence!

Pray: Lord, help me to gratefully acknowledge your presence with ever deepening trust and faith. Amen.

Reflect

_____
_____
_____
_____
_____
_____
_____
_____
_____
_____
_____
_____
_____
_____
_____
_____
_____
_____
_____
_____
_____
_____
_____
_____
_____
_____
_____
_____
_____

Day 13

✑

The Divine Teacher

Read: John 3:2-21

... unless one is born of water and the Spirit, he cannot enter the kingdom of God. (v. 5 ESV)

Sometimes the only way to save a plant is to uproot it and find a heartier place for it to grow. Otherwise, the plant will wither and die without producing the harvest it was intended to create. I'm no green thumb, but at a minimum I understand the theory!

When Jesus suggested to Nicodemus, "unless a man is born again, he cannot see the kingdom of God" (v. 3), he was teaching him a basic faith lesson. Nicodemus' essence as a man wouldn't change in this process, but his spiritual rebirth would transform his heart and usher in a new way of living. In order for his life to be saved, Nicodemus needed to be transplanted through water and the Spirit. Then and only then would he enter the kingdom.

New believers are like tender re-potted plantings of the Lord. They need lots of love and attention if they are to continue to grow and bear fruit. The Gospels are replete with the divine teachings of Christ and are the best nourishment for feeding all re-born, re-potted souls. Is there someone within your reach that needs some tender loving kingdom care today?

Pray: Lord Jesus, teach me your truth today so that the roots of my faith will grow deeply into the soil of your love.

Reflect

_____

_____

_____

_____

_____

_____

_____

_____

_____

_____

_____

_____

_____

_____

_____

_____

_____

_____

_____

_____

_____

_____

_____

_____

_____

_____

_____

Day 14

❧

The Soul Winner

Read: John 4:7-29

... but whoever drinks of the water that I will give him will never be thirsty again. The water that I will give him will become in him a spring of water welling up to eternal life. (v. 14 ESV)

It was a divine appointment and Jesus took advantage of it. The Samaritan woman happened upon the well where Jesus was resting, and the water she came to draw produced within her a wellspring of eternal life. She found living water on that day and her life would never be the same again.

Can you recall the day you first discovered

the difference between a self-centered and a God-centered life? Did you meet him along the roadside of your life where you were stunned by his loving, merciful knowledge of every thought you held so near?

The Samaritan woman was startled to find a man–a Jew, no less!–who knew so much about her and yet cared so deeply for her. Jesus knew all about her spotty past and was there to invite her into a forgiven present and worshipful future. He won over this woman's soul through his gentle tenacity.

Jesus is a soul winner. It's an old-fashioned expression but a very present reality. Unless he's won yours, you aren't really his. Soul winner is he .... and soul winners are we.

Pray: Lord, give me the courageous joy and grace to boldly proclaim your love to all who cross my path today.

Reflect

_____
_____
_____
_____
_____
_____
_____
_____
_____
_____
_____
_____
_____
_____
_____
_____
_____
_____
_____
_____
_____
_____
_____
_____
_____
_____
_____
_____

Day 15

❦

The Great Physician

Read: John 5:1-15

Do you want to be healed? ... Get up, take up your bed, and walk. (vv. 6, 8 ESV)

Who wouldn't want to get well? It's a strange question indeed, but Jesus started with it to begin the physical and spiritual healing this invalid needed. If the man didn't want to get well (because he was too worn down by suffering ... too comfortable with his affliction ... too dependent on the pity of others) then perhaps Jesus would not have healed him.

In mercy Jesus invites the man to pick up his mat and walk. Jesus the Great Physician touched this invalid after 38 years of suffering and brought about the joy of miraculous healing.

Eleven times over seventeen years we offered our son into the hands of surgeons as they tried everything possible to strengthen a weak tibia in his right leg. Each time we yearned and prayed for healing but it didn't come until after the twelfth surgery. We have no idea why it took so long, but we claim his healing in the name of the Great Physician.

Trust him to heal you when and as he desires. Meanwhile, ask God to heal you spiritually so that you are his no matter what.

Pray: I trust you, Jesus, to heal my heart, and if it's your will, to heal my body too.

Reflect

_____

_____

_____

_____

_____

_____

_____

_____

_____

_____

_____

_____

_____

_____

_____

_____

_____

_____

_____

_____

_____

_____

_____

_____

_____

_____

Day 16

❦

The Bread of Life

Read: John 6:32-58

I am the bread of life; whoever comes to me shall not hunger, and whoever believes in me shall never thirst. (v. 35 ESV)

Spiritual anemia is a problem in the church today. Many who claim the name of Christ have actually stagnated in their growth as believers. The church doesn't have any appeal to them, and they can't recall the last time they've opened the Bible or devoted any significant time to prayer.

In this passage Jesus reminds his disciples that he is the Bread of Life. Feed on him and you will experience the abundance of eternal life. "For on him God the Father has set his seal." (John 6:27 ESV). Therefore, if we come to him and believe in him we will never be spiritually hungry again!

Feeding on Christ and his Word is like enjoying a midnight buffet on the finest of cruise ships. The extravagant feast is so overwhelming that you will never consume it all. You keep coming back for more, and finding there is always more to receive.

Come to the table and enjoy the Bread of Life. Your soul will never go hungry. Invite others to the table and share the feast, for there's enough of him to feed the whole world.

Pray: Lord, I am hungry for your love, mercy, tenderness, and grace. Feed my soul with the bread of life.

Reflect

_____

_____

_____

_____

_____

_____

_____

_____

_____

_____

_____

_____

_____

_____

_____

_____

_____

_____

_____

_____

_____

_____

_____

_____

_____

Day 17

❧

The Water of Life

Read: John 7:25-44

If anyone thirsts, let him come to me and drink. Whoever believes in me, as the Scripture has said, "Out of his heart will flow rivers of living water." (vv. 37-38 ESV)

Stationed along marathon routes are people handing cups of water to runners in need of sustenance for the miles ahead. Those on the sidelines are literally "pouring courage" into the hearts and bodies of those pounding along their lengthy route. If it weren't for the water, the runner would dehydrate, collapse, and fall out of the race.

When we come to Jesus and drink deeply from the water of life he offers, we are replenished for the day ahead. We come to him with a craving thirst, knowing that he will satisfy our soul. He has never disappointed his children by withholding streams of living water.

The water Jesus gives is found in his Word, demonstrated in his love, and confirmed in prayer. He not only gives it to us individually but corporately, within the faith community of the church. We can drink from this spring alone and together, and the refreshment of Christ's life sustains us for the road ahead.

Don't try running life's race without the living water of Christ ... otherwise you will tire and fall.

Pray: Lord, I come with mouth wide open to drink in your love today. Satisfy my thirst like only you can do!

Reflect

Day 18

❧

The Defender
of the Weak

Read: John 8:3-11

Let him who is without sin among you be the first to throw a stone at her. (v. 5 ESV)

The neighborhood bully is always picking on the weakest in the bunch. We had one in our community and everyone stayed away from him, not just the scrawny kids who lived in fear of him. The resident bully liked to belittle the weak and intimidate all who stood in his way.

In bringing a woman caught in adultery to Jesus for judgment, the Pharisees and the teachers of the law weren't really seeking justice. This was a ploy, a tactic they were using to entrap Jesus. What did he think of this woman? Would he condemn her and gain a reputation for harshness, or release her and show himself soft on sin?

Instead of a direct answer to their question, Jesus writes on the ground with his finger and then stands up straight with a retort that caught them off guard, "If any one of you is without sin, let him be the first to throw a stone at her." One by one they all disappeared without a word–or a stone.

How we treat sinners should be a reflection of Jesus' defense of love. Jesus urged the woman to leave her life of sin with tenderness–no bullying required!

Pray: Thank you, Jesus, for defending the weak and sinful–yes, even me.

Reflect

Day 19

∞

The Light of the World

Read John 9:1-39

As long as I am in the world, I am the light of the world. (v. 5 ESV)

Lighthouses are firmly planted in strategic locations along dark and rocky shorelines. They are positioned there to provide much needed warning and guidance to ships at sea. Even their faint hints of light from miles off shore provide direction to vessels in search of safe passage and home port.

When Jesus walked this earth, he was himself a

bright beacon of light in a dark and needy world. His light shone brilliantly every place he went, particularly for those who were hopeless, hungry, or hurting.

In this passage, we witness once more the compassion of Christ displayed. Sent by Jesus to wash in the pool of Siloam, the blind man returned home seeing. He had been healed of his infirmity and for the first time in his life he had the joy of beholding the light of the world.

Jesus is the Light of the World. His presence shines brightly before us as we seek safe harbor and follow his way home. As you come alongside others who are walking in darkness today, encourage them to trust the light of Christ.

Pray: May the light of Christ guard my heart, guide my way, and gracefully lead others to safe harbor. Amen.

Reflect

_____
_____
_____
_____
_____
_____
_____
_____
_____
_____
_____
_____
_____
_____
_____
_____
_____
_____
_____
_____
_____
_____
_____
_____
_____
_____
_____
_____
_____

Day 20

⌇

The Good Shepherd

Read: John 10:1-16

I am the good shepherd. I know my own and my own know me ... and I lay down my life for the sheep. (vv. 14, 15 ESV)

"I came that they may have life and have it abundantly." (John 10:10 ESV), says Jesus the Good Shepherd. Providing pasture that breeds life is exactly what he did for his disciples ... and precisely what he wants us to do for others.

A good shepherd leads his sheep into safe pasture, where nourishment is plentiful and where protective oversight can be preserved. It requires that the shepherd be compassionate, courageous, tough, and tender. Even to the point of willingly risking his life to provide for the sheep.

Jesus gave his life so that we can have ours. It's that simple and it's that profound. He willingly laid down his life and suffered on our behalf so that we could be delivered from the confusion and death of sin into the redeemed life of his flock. He calls us to that same sacrificial service on behalf of all who are in our flock.

The Good Shepherd sacrificially gave up his life so his sheep can live abundantly. In light of that gospel reality, be sure to trust the leading of the Shepherd. His care for your soul is eternal.

Pray: Guide me into safe pasture and shepherd me with your loving kindness as I put my complete trust in you, Lord Jesus.

Reflect

_____
_____
_____
_____
_____
_____
_____
_____
_____
_____
_____
_____
_____
_____
_____
_____
_____
_____
_____
_____
_____
_____
_____
_____

Day 21

⚜

The Resurrection
and the Life

Read: John 11:1-44

I am the resurrection and the life. Whoever believes in me, though he die, yet shall he live. (v. 25 ESV)

Jesus wept. He loved Lazarus. He wanted to be there for Mary and Martha. Then Jesus raised Lazarus from the dead, not out of a selfish desire for his company or even to show off his miraculous abilities. Jesus set Lazarus free from his grave clothes to display the glory of God.

Lazarus had already been in the tomb for

four days. The mourners had come to comfort his sisters, who believed that had Jesus only been there on time, their brother would not have died. Meanwhile, Martha was on the hunt for Jesus. After she found him, Jesus set out to wake his beloved friend who had fallen into death's sleep.

Christ's awesome power dispels the darkness of death. "I am the resurrection and the life," Jesus told Martha. "Do you believe this?" "Yes, Lord, I believe that you are the Christ, the Son of God."

Those who believe in the resurrection and the life will never die, in the sense that earthly death leads us into God's presence. Do you believe him today? If so, then express your heart of love and gratitude to the Lord and be sure to share that love with all who have yet to believe.

Pray: Lord, I trust you today to reveal your love. Open the eyes of my heart to see your glory!

Reflect

_____
_____
_____
_____
_____
_____
_____
_____
_____
_____
_____
_____
_____
_____
_____
_____
_____
_____
_____
_____
_____
_____
_____
_____
_____
_____
_____

Day 22

❦

The King

Read: John 12:1-15

Hosanna! Blessed is he who comes in the name of the Lord, even the King of Israel! (v. 13 ESV)

Imagine the curiosity of the people who went to look at Jesus and Lazarus, the man whom he had raised from the dead. Who wouldn't want to see such a spectacle? Is it any wonder, therefore, that the growing crowd who had gathered for the Passover Feast the very next day would take palm branches and meet Jesus with shouts of "Hosanna!"

For this short-lived moment, the crowds had

indeed thought they had encountered their king. As Jesus entered Jerusalem riding a young donkey and cheered on by the crowd, the Pharisees watched with horror at what seemed like the whole world going after him!

Mary had it right all along. In John 12:3 we see her pouring out a pint of expensive perfume on the feet of Jesus. The whole house was filled with the wonderful fragrance. Despite the disgust of Judas, everyone else must have enjoyed the aroma of his divine presence.

His kingly rule is for our hearts forever, not for the stirring up of a temporary enthusiasm that only lasts a moment. Worship the King in all his splendor. Begin by pouring out all that you have at his feet. He will wipe away all of your tears.

Pray: Lord, help me to build your kingdom today, beginning in my heart.

Reflect

_____
_____
_____
_____
_____
_____
_____
_____
_____
_____
_____
_____
_____
_____
_____
_____
_____
_____
_____
_____
_____
_____
_____
_____
_____
_____
_____
_____

Day 23

⚬

The Servant

Read John 13:1-17

... having loved his own who were in the world, he loved them to the end. (v. 1 ESV)

One of the final and most intimate moments Jesus spent with his disciples took place in the Upper Room during the last supper. It included his pouring water into a basin, washing, and drying their feet.

Peter was obviously not prepared for this. His sense of unworthiness held him back from receiving the humble service of the Master. Jesus responded to Peter's objection by stating, "If I do not wash you, you have no share with me."(v.

8), and with that Peter asked to be cleansed from head to toe!

Receiving the service of others can be hard for those generally accustomed to giving–moms and dads, ministers and missionaries, just to name a few. For the disciples, they had witnessed a constant flow of service from Christ. With their feet held graciously in his hands, he called them to do likewise for others.

How willing are you to serve as a living example of Christ? Whose feet (literally or figuratively) need to be held in your hands, washed, and wiped clean by the power of love, grace, mercy, and forgiveness? Serve in his name and watch the transformation of heart that will follow.

Pray: Lord, I desire to follow your example–lead me to the one you call me to serve today.

Reflect

_____

_____

_____

_____

_____

_____

_____

_____

_____

_____

_____

_____

_____

_____

_____

_____

_____

_____

_____

_____

_____

_____

_____

_____

Day 24

❧

The Great Consoler

Read: John 14:1-14

L et not your hearts be troubled. Believe in God; believe also in me. (v. 1 ESV)

The night was dark and frightful. As the thunder clapped and the lightning lit up the sky, I held my daughter firmly on my lap. I too was a bit overwhelmed by the drama, but we rocked and sang and whispered words of love. There was comfort and peace within us and as a result, we were not shattered by the noise of the night all around us.

Jesus consoles his disciples as his departure draws near. Thomas and Philip want to know where he is going (John 14:5) and who will show them the way (v. 8). Jesus' answers bring them back to the simple truths he's told them all along the way: "Don't let your hearts be troubled; trust in God; have faith in me."

When the journey of life becomes dark and difficult, and you seem to have lost your way, you are only a short prayer away from the Great Consoler. Jesus–the way, the truth and the life–invites us to lean on him for strength.

Trust in God's abiding presence. The noise of the day or the darkness of night will not keep him from coming to you with his love and comfort.

Pray: Lord Jesus, I wholeheartedly desire your truth and life ... please show me the way.

Reflect

_____
_____
_____
_____
_____
_____
_____
_____
_____
_____
_____
_____
_____
_____
_____
_____
_____
_____
_____
_____
_____
_____
_____
_____
_____
_____
_____
_____

Day 25

&cpsw;

The True Vine

Read: John 15:1-17

Abide in me, and I in you. (v. 4 ESV)

Garden imagery is a favorite of God's ... from the creation story Garden of Eden to the well-watered garden of the prophets to the Garden of Gethsemane where Jesus prays. In John 15, Jesus reminds his disciples of the Father as gardener of their hearts.

He teaches the disciples that every branch of his that bears no fruit, the Father will cut off; while every branch that does bear fruit, the Father will trim clean so it will become even more fruitful!

The main idea is simply this: no lonely, cutoff branch can bear fruit by itself; it must remain in the vine.

What is the fruit that the Father desires of his children? Jesus tells us that it begins with obeying his commands and it's evidenced by remaining true to his wish, "love one another as I have loved you" (15:12 NIV).

The fruit of love begins to grow with daily prayer and reflection on the Word of God. It flourishes in our relationships with our family, friends, neighbors, and work associates. It bursts into full bloom when we're confronted with a difficult person and we reflect Jesus' heart and mind.

But it can all quickly wither when we fail to abide in Christ.

Pray: Lord, help me to abide in you, and to love all others in your name.

Reflect

_____

_____

_____

_____

_____

_____

_____

_____

_____

_____

_____

_____

_____

_____

_____

_____

_____

_____

_____

_____

_____

_____

_____

_____

_____

_____

Day 26

❦

The Giver of the
Holy Spirit

Read: John 16:1-16

When the Spirit of truth comes, he will guide you into all the truth. (v. 14 ESV)

Perhaps the saddest story related to the aftermath of the devastating tsunami in southeast Asia is the thousands of children left as orphans. Their villages, homes, and families were washed away with the overpowering waves that came crashing on shore. In one terrible instant these children's lives were changed forever.

Jesus promised his disciples that he would not

leave them as orphans (John 14:18). Out of great love for his disciples, Jesus pledged the gift of the Holy Spirit to be with them forever. Described as the Spirit of truth, the Spirit is ready to provide all that his role is intended—to comfort them in their loss, to convict them of their sin, and to guide them into all truth. In all of this the Spirit will bring glory to God.

We can be comforted in the reality of this promise as his disciples today. We will never be left as orphans. No matter the condition of our lives or the state of our circumstances, the Spirit has come to give us life and hope in all its abundance. As a result, our grief will be transformed into complete joy—now and for all eternity!

Pray: For the glory of your name, come Holy Spirit and make your empowering presence known to all of your children worldwide.

Reflect

_____

_____

_____

_____

_____

_____

_____

_____

_____

_____

_____

_____

_____

_____

_____

_____

_____

_____

_____

_____

_____

_____

_____

_____

_____

Day 27

❦

The Great Intercessor

Read: John 17:1-26

... that they may become perfectly one, so that the world may know that you sent me and loved them even as you loved me. (v. 23 ESV)

Do you know anyone you would consider a committed prayer warrior–perhaps a parent, pastor, or friend? No matter how great their prayer life, their example is merely a faint reflection of the devotion Jesus showed in his own prayer life.

John 17 is the apex of Jesus' modeling of intercessory prayer. He starts with a focus on the glory of God, from before the world began until the Son of God graced this earth (vv. 1-5). This leads into prayer for his immediate band of disciples, for their protection, joy, and sanctification (vv. 6-19). Jesus concludes with appeals for all believers of every generation, praying for their unity, their devotion to his mission, and to one another (vv. 20-26). All of this for the glory of God!

In your intercession for those in your sphere of influence, take seriously the example of the Master. He will teach you to pray and will gently invite you into the themes he spells out so clearly in this passage. The best way for the world to believe in the Savior is through the unity of God's praying people.

Pray: Lord Jesus, let your light shine brightly in my prayer closet and gloriously throughout this world.

Reflect

_____
_____
_____
_____
_____
_____
_____
_____
_____
_____
_____
_____
_____
_____
_____
_____
_____
_____
_____
_____
_____
_____
_____
_____
_____

Day 28

⚮

The Model Sufferer

Read: John 18:1-11

Put your sword into its sheath; shall I not drink the cup that the Father has given me? (v. 11 ESV)

In an olive grove called the Garden of Gethsemane the drama began to unfold. There Christ is confronted by his betrayer and a detachment of soldiers. They are in search of Jesus of Nazareth and he willingly responds with the simple words, "I am he."

In tempestuous anger, Peter draws his sword and cuts off the high priest's servant's ear. But Jesus silences the altercation by commanding Peter to put his sword away. Willingly Christ drinks the cup of suffering given to him by the Father.

I'm not one for embracing suffering, especially if I know it's coming my way. I dodge it, avoid it, minimize it ... but rarely will I embrace it. One mentor encouraged me in the midst of a violent relational storm, "Someday you will be thankful for this season of suffering." It took a few months, but eventually I saw his wisdom. I grew stronger by drinking the cup that was given to me.

In the midst of the suffering that led to his death on the cross, Jesus embraced the Father's will. It was his most important decision–and our most life-transforming reward. Choose life, even when suffering comes along as its natural companion.

Pray: Remind me of your willingness to suffer when I am confronted with heartache.

Reflect

_____

_____

_____

_____

_____

_____

_____

_____

_____

_____

_____

_____

_____

_____

_____

_____

_____

_____

_____

_____

_____

_____

_____

_____

Day 29

❧

The Uplifted Savior

Read: John 19:1-19

So he [Pilate] delivered him [Jesus] over to them to be crucified. (v. 16 ESV)

Flogged, humiliated, and wearing a crown of thorns on his head, Jesus was taken away to be crucified. Carrying his own cross, he was sent through the city streets to Golgotha, "The Place of the Skull." There he hung on the cross with the notice fastened above his head, "Jesus of Nazareth, The King of the Jews."

Uplifted on a cross? Yes, to a wooden cross he was fastened and lifted up to die. There he would suffer for our iniquities, once and for all time he would seal his role as our Savior. No more need to sacrifice animals and offer their bodies in our behalf. Christ the Lord, the uplifted Savior, has taken our sin and our shame and redeemed us on the cross.

What is your response to his crucifixion? Are you horrified or grateful or maybe both? When I first saw Mel Gibson's movie The Passion of the Christ I was both. The vivid portrayal of the flogging, painful crowning, and humiliating agony of the cross all evoked deeply felt emotion. In the midst of my tears, I was both saddened and thankful.

The uplifted Savior is worthy of our praise and worship. "Love's redeeming work is done; fought the fight, the battle's won, Alleluia!"

Pray: May the grateful response of my heart be pleasing in your sight, O divine Savior!

Reflect

_____
_____
_____
_____
_____
_____
_____
_____
_____
_____
_____
_____
_____
_____
_____
_____
_____
_____
_____
_____
_____
_____
_____
_____
_____
_____

Day 30

The Conqueror of Death

Read: John 20:1-31

Put your finger here, and see my hands; and put out your hand, and place it in my side. Do not disbelieve, but believe. (v. 27 ESV)

The first Easter must have been glorious! Mary of Magdala is the first to discover the empty tomb. She runs to Peter and John the beloved disciple and they in turn run back to the tomb and believe. The risen Christ appears to Mary who was sitting outside the tomb in tears. Then he appears to 10 of his disciples that evening. Everyone in the room receives his peace and the breath of the Holy Spirit.

Judas the betrayer was one of the disciples missing out on this joyful encounter. The other was Thomas the doubter. Even when Thomas heard about the meeting, he held out in disbelief. A week later, when Jesus arrived among the disciples Thomas gets to reach out and touch the risen Christ for himself, and he exclaims, "My Lord and my God!"

Are you filled with joy in the reality of loving, worshiping, and serving the conqueror of death, the risen and majestic Lord? This story was written so that we may believe in the Son of God and have life in his name (v. 31). We too will die, yet shall we live–all because Jesus conquered death once and for all.

Pray: Renew my zeal to run with faith and strength toward the risen Christ. Amen.

Reflect

_____

_____

_____

_____

_____

_____

_____

_____

_____

_____

_____

_____

_____

_____

_____

_____

_____

_____

_____

_____

_____

_____

_____

_____

_____

_____

_____

Day 31

Day 31

✑

The Restorer of the Penitent

Read: John 21:1-19

... do you love me more than these? ... Tend my sheep ... Follow me. (vv. 15, 16, 19 ESV)

How many times did Jesus have to ask Peter if he truly loved him? Apparently three, or at least that's the minimum number recorded for us to consider! Of course Jesus knew his heart better than Peter could imagine, but in the affirmative responses Peter's affections were sealed by the spoken word.

For Jesus, the beginning point is the verbal

witness. The expression of love must be generated at the street level of service. Jesus tells Peter to "feed my lambs" and "take care of my sheep" and "feed my sheep" as specific indicators of his overarching command to "follow me."

When we follow Christ we are invited into a deep and profound relationship with him. He delights to restore those who are penitent so that we may serve him with ever increasing joy and effectiveness. He wants our hearts first, then our lips to give voice to our commitment, followed by a lifetime of faithful service.

Jesus is asking for your verbal declaration of love. Then he wants to know how willing you are to sacrificially serve him. It may require that you are led to places you would rather not go, but that's what this life of faith is all about.

Pray: Lord, I choose to love and follow you today and forever.

Reflect

_____

_____

_____

_____

_____

_____

_____

_____

_____

_____

_____

_____

_____

_____

_____

_____

_____

_____

_____

_____

_____

_____

_____

_____

About the Author

Stephen A. Macchia is the founding president of Leadership Transformations, Inc. (LTI), a ministry focusing on the spiritual formation needs of leaders and the spiritual discernment processes of leadership teams in local church and parachurch ministry settings. In conjunction with his leadership of LTI, he also serves as the director of the Pierce Center for Disciple-Building at Gordon-Conwell Theological Seminary. He is the author of several books, including *Becoming a Healthy Church, Becoming a Healthy Disciple, Becoming A Healthy Team*, and *Crafting A Rule of Life*. Stephen and his wife, Ruth, are the proud parents of Nathan and Rebekah and reside in Lexington, Massachusetts.

For more information about Stephen A. Macchia or Leadership Transformations, Inc., visit:

www.LeadershipTransformations.org
www.HealthyChurch.net
www.RuleOfLife.com

Other Titles by Stephen A. Macchia

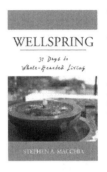

The Bible is filled with more than 50 different depictions of the heart, such as hardened, humble, deceitful and grateful. God's desire is to woo his followers to devote their whole heart to him in all aspects of their personal life and worship: loving God with "all" their heart…as well as with their soul, mind, and strength.

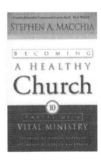

In **Becoming a Healthy Church**, Stephen A. Macchia illustrates how to move beyond church growth to church health. Healthy growth is a process that requires risk taking, lifestyle changes, and ongoing evaluation. This book is a practical, hands-on manual to launch you and your church into a process of positive change. Available in 4 Languages: English, Chinese, Korean, Spanish.

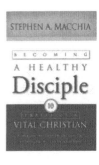

Becoming a Healthy Disciple explores the ten traits of a healthy disciple, including a vital prayer life, evangelistic outreach, worship, servanthood, and stewardship. He applies to individual Christians the ten characteristics of a healthy church outlined in his previous book, *Becoming a Healthy Church*. Discipleship is a lifelong apprenticeship to Jesus Christ, the master teacher. Macchia looks to John the beloved disciple as an example of a life lived close to Christ.

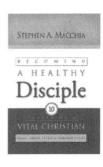

Becoming a Healthy Disciple Small Group Study & Worship Guide is a companion to Steve Macchia's book, *Becoming a Healthy Disciple*. This small group guide provides discussion and worship outlines to enrich your study of the ten traits of a healthy disciple. This 12-week small group resource provides Study, Worship, and Prayer guidelines for each session.

Becoming a Healthy Team is essential for building the kingdom. Stephen A. Macchia offers tried and tested principles and practices to help your leadership team do the same. He'll show you how to Trust, Empower, Assimilate, Manage, and Serve. That spells TEAMS and ultimately success. Filled with scriptural guideposts, *Becoming a Healthy Team* provides practical answers and pointed questions to keep your team on track and moving ahead.

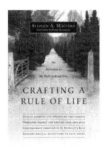

In **Crafting a Rule of Life** Stephen A. Macchia looks to St. Benedict as a guide for discovering your own rule of life in community. It is a process that takes time and concerted effort; you must listen to God and discern what he wants you to be and do for his glory. But through the basic disciplines of Scripture, prayer and reflection in a small group context this practical workbook will lead you forward in a journey toward Christlikeness.

Additional Resouces @
SPIRITUALFORMATIONSTORE.COM

Guide to Prayer for All Who Walk With God

The latest from Rueben Job, A Guide to Prayer for All Who Walk With God offers a simple pattern of daily prayer built around weekly themes and organized by the Christian church year. Each week features readings for reflection from such well-known spiritual writers as Francis of Assisi, Teresa of Avila, Dietrich Bonhoeffer, Henri J. M. Nouwen, Sue Monk Kidd, Martin Luther, Julian of Norwich, M. Basil Pennington, Evelyn Underhill, Douglas Steere, and many others.

Guide to Prayer for All Who Seek God

For nearly 20 years, people have turned to the Guide to Prayer series for a daily rhythm of devotion and personal worship. Thousands of readers appreciate the series' simple structure of daily worship, rich spiritual writings, lectionary guidelines, and poignant prayers. Like its predecessors, A Guide to Prayer for All Who Seek God will become a treasured favorite for those hungering for God as the Christian year unfolds.

Guide to Prayer for Ministers and Other Servants

A best-seller for more than a decade! This classic devotional and prayer book includes thematically arranged material for each week of the year as well as themes and schedules for 12 personal retreats. The authors have adopted the following daily format for this prayer book: daily invocations, readings, scripture, reflection, prayers, weekly hymns, benedictions, and printed psalms.

Guide to Prayer for All God's People

A compilation of scripture, prayers and spiritual readings, this inexhaustible resource contains thematically arranged material for each week of the year and for monthly personal retreats. Its contents have made it a sought-after desk reference, a valuable library resource and a cherished companion.

LEADERSHIP
TRANSFORMATIONS _{INC.}

FORMATION | DISCERNMENT | RENEWAL

- Soul Care Retreats and Soul Sabbaths
- Emmaus: Spiritual Leadership Communities
- Selah: Spiritual Direction Certificate Program
- Spiritual Formation Groups
- Spiritual Health Assessments
- Spiritual Discernment for Teams
- Sabbatical Planning
- Spiritual Formation Resources

Visit www.LeadershipTransformations.org

or call (877) TEAM LTI

Made in the USA
Columbia, SC
05 December 2022

72775818R00078